NATIONAL GEOGRAPHIC

Return to
Titanic

PIONEER EDITION

By Susan E. Goodman

CONTENTS

Re

Pieces of the Past. *Rust clings to Titanic's bow, the pointed front of the ship. OPPOSITE PAGE: In 1912, this watch was found on the body of a passenger.*

rn to Titanic

Titanic was meant to be the biggest and best ship of her day. Then she sank in 1912. Yet she is still the most famous boat on Earth.

By
Susan E. Goodman

Sailing Into History.
Passengers stand along Titanic's stern, or back.

The Wonder Ship

Crowds of people packed a dock in England. It was April 10, 1912.

They had come to see *Titanic*. This ship was about to leave on her first trip. And what a ship she was!

Titanic was huge. She was the largest ship in the world. She was as long as four city blocks.

Titanic was also a floating palace. She had a pool. She had gold lights and carved wood. She also had many rich and famous passengers. They wanted to be the first to ride on this great ship.

Danger Ahead!

Titanic set off for New York. At first, the ride was like a party. By April 14, the ship was in the middle of the Atlantic Ocean.

That night, the weather was clear. Stars twinkled in the sky. On the ship, people danced late into the night. No one knew danger was near.

Then a sailor saw an **iceberg.** That is a floating mountain of ice. He raised the alarm: "Iceberg ahead!"

The crew tried to turn *Titanic* away. But it was too late. The ship scraped along the ice.

Water Rushes In

The problem did not seem too bad at first. Then water started pouring in. Nothing could stop it. The ship was going to sink!

The crew tried to get help. They shot off fireworks. Other ships thought the fireworks were for fun. They did not stop to help.

People climbed into lifeboats. Women and children mostly went first. There was not enough room for everyone. The last boat left. Yet 1,500 people were still on the sinking ship.

HULTON ARCHIVE, GETTY IMAGES; ILLUSTRATION BY KEN MARSCHALL © 1992 FROM TITANIC: AN ILLUSTRATED HISTORY, A HYPERION/MADISON PRESS BOOK

A Ship Torn Apart

Soon passengers heard a terrible sound. The ship was ripping apart. It sank 20 minutes later. Most of the passengers and crew were still on board. They went down with the ship.

Breaking News. *A newsboy sells papers in London. The ship's sinking shocked people around the world.*

Unhappy Ending. *The Titanic breaks apart just a few minutes before sinking to the seafloor.*

From the Deep. *Bob Ballard and a crew member sit in their ship's control room. They are watching images of an anchor from* Titanic.

A Boy's Dream

Titanic sank to the ocean floor. It stayed there for 71 years. Then Robert Ballard set out to find her.

As a kid, Ballard had loved reading about *Titanic.* "My dream," he says, "was to find this great ship."

Ballard became an ocean explorer. He studied the ocean floor. He made many discoveries. But he never forgot his dream. He still wanted to find *Titanic.*

People said it was impossible. The shipwreck was too deep. Ballard did not agree.

Hunting for Titanic

In 1985, Ballard began his search. He teamed up with a French scientist. They took ships to where *Titanic* had sunk. They used high-tech tools to search the ocean floor. For weeks, they found nothing.

Then they sent down *Argo.* It was an underwater machine. It took pictures and sent them back.

Argo searched the ocean for a few days. Still nothing. Then a big metal object came into view. It was a ship's engine. The team began to cheer. They had found *Titanic!*

A Closer Look

Ballard saw *Titanic*'s **bow,** or front. It was stuck in mud. He saw cups and beds. Ballard also saw shoes and suitcases.

It was like visiting a museum. Ballard wanted to see more. But he had run out of time. He had to return home.

In 1986, Ballard came back to the ship. This time, he traveled down to the wreck. He rode in a **submersible,** or an underwater craft. He brought a deep-sea robot. The robot took a look inside the ship.

Saving the Past

Ballard explored *Titanic*. He took pictures of the shipwreck. He gave people new views of the ship.

But Ballard did not take anything away. He left things just as they were. Each object helps to tell the sad story of *Titanic*.

Wordwise

bow: front of a ship

iceberg: floating mountain of ice

submersible: underwater craft

Talking With Bob Ba

lard

"I'm more than just the *Titanic* guy," says Bob Ballard. He is right about that. Ballard has explored many parts of the ocean. In this interview, he talks about his work.

How did you get interested in ocean exploration?

I always loved the book *Twenty Thousand Leagues Under the Sea* by Jules Verne. It was all I could think about. I wanted to see what was deep in the ocean!

How did you become an ocean explorer?

I was lucky. I grew up in a smart family. My parents wanted me to have a good education. I went to college and studied the ocean. Later, I joined the Navy. I became an ocean explorer.

There have been many shipwrecks. What is special about *Titanic*?

Titanic's story interests people. The ship was full of people when it sank. Many were scared. Many were brave. Many were also very famous. People want to hear their stories.

People also like robots. They want to know how we study the shipwreck. They want to learn about our work.

PRIIT VESILIND

Deep Discoveries. ABOVE: *Bob Ballard is an ocean explorer.* LEFT: *Submersibles like ALVIN help Ballard explore the deep ocean.*

Why is it a bad idea to take items from the wreck?

The objects are part of history. Seeing them in place tells a lot. For example, we can learn how the ship sank. That information is lost if you take things away from the wreck.

What was it like to find *Titanic?* How did you feel?

Finding *Titanic* was a dream of mine. So discovering it made me happy. Yet some of my other work is more important. My biggest discovery was even deeper in the ocean. I found life around cracks in the ocean floor.

What are you exploring now?

I am excited about underwater archaeology. That is the study of underwater objects. They help us learn about people who lived long ago. I am now exploring the Black Sea and the Aegean Sea. They are full of ancient shipwrecks.

What would you tell kids who want to become ocean explorers?

Study hard. Take classes in everything you can. Experiment. Test things. Do not worry about mistakes. You can learn from them. If you fall down, get back up. Follow your dreams!

Exploring the Deep

Ballard has made many discoveries. He found life where no one thought it could be *(above)*. Today, Ballard explores ancient shipwrecks *(top and right)*. Robot subs help him learn about people of the past.

Ancient History. *This jar from a shipwreck tells about past cultures.* LEFT: *Ballard found this pile of jars in the Black Sea. It is part of a shipwreck.*

New Technology. *The robot sub, Jason, has a movable arm. The arm lets Ballard lift and study the objects in ancient shipwrecks.*

Exploring Titanic

It is time to dive in and see what you have learned.

 Why did many famous people want to ride on *Titanic*?

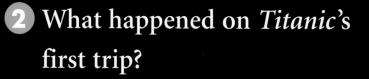 What happened on *Titanic*'s first trip?

 How did Bob Ballard explore *Titanic*? What did he find?

4 Why is it wrong to take things from a shipwreck?

5 Would you like to be an ocean explorer? Why or why not?